TRUE CRIME

Cyber Crime

John Townsend

Raintree

www.raintreepublishers.co.uk

Visit our website to find out more information about **Raintree** books.

To order:
☎ Phone 44 (0) 1865 888113
▤ Send a fax to 44 (0) 1865 314091
▱ Visit the Raintree Bookshop at **www.raintreepublishers.co.uk** to browse our catalogue and order online.

First published in Great Britain by
Raintree, Halley Court, Jordan Hill, Oxford OX2 8EJ,
part of Harcourt Education.
Raintree is a registered trademark of Harcourt
Education Ltd.

Editorial: Melanie Copland and
Kate Buckingham
Design: Michelle Lisseter and Kamae Design
Picture Research: Maria Joannou and
Ginny Stroud-Lewis
Index: Indexing Specialists (UK) Ltd
Production: Duncan Gilbert

Originated by Dot Gradations Ltd
Printed and bound in China
by South China Printing Company

ISBN 1 844 43589 X (hardback)
08 07 06 05 04
10 9 8 7 6 5 4 3 2 1

ISBN 1 844 43595 4 (paperback)
09 08 07 06 05
10 9 8 7 6 5 4 3 2 1

British Library Cataloguing in Publication Data
Townsend, John
Cyber crime – (True Crime)
364.1'68

A full catalogue record for this book is available from
the British Library.

Acknowledgements
Alamy pp. **13, 34, 19** (Don Tremain), **22** (Image
source), **11** (Mike Hill), **8** (National Motor Museum);
Associated Press pp. **9, 18, 38–39, 16** (Canadian
Press/Andre Forget); Corbis pp. **20, 32, 36–37** (Bill
Stormont), **35** (Charles O'Rear), **29** (Chris Hardy/San
Francisco Chronicle), **38** (Gregory Pace), **22–23, 25,
30, 42,** (Harcourt Education Ltd), **27** (Jose Fuste
Raga), **37** (Leif Skoogfors), **10–11** (Pete Saloutos);
Corbis Sygma pp. **14–15** (Gordon Chet), **9** (J Bounds-
RNO); PA Photos p. **34**; Photodisc/ Harcourt
Education Ltd pp. **4–5, 5, 14, 16–17, 21, 32–33, 41,
43**; Ronald Grant archive pp. **6–7**; Science Photo
Library pp. **12** (Andrew Syred), **33** (BSIP Laurent/H
Amerciain), **7** (Jerry Mason), **42–43** (Martin Dohrn),
12–13 (Victor Habbrok Visuals); The Kobal
Collection pp. **6, 24, 32–33** (Mayfair/Transcas),
30–31 Paramount/Gordon, Melinda Sue); Tudor
Photography pp. **28, 40–41**.

Cover photograph of man at computer reproduced
with permission of Corbis/Hermann/Starke

Disclaimer
All the Internet addresses (URLs) given in this book
were valid at the time of going to press. However, due
to the dynamic nature of the Internet, some addresses
may have changed, or sites may have changed or
ceased to exist since publication. While the author and
publishers regret any inconvenience this may cause
readers, no responsibility for any such changes can be
accepted by either the author or the publishers.

Contents

Any words appearing in the text in bold, **like this,** are explained in the Glossary. You can also look out for them in the Word Bank at the bottom of each page.

Open doors

Whether a door is open, closed or locked, a thief will try to get inside. That may mean:
- stepping through an open doorway
- turning the handle and pushing it open
- breaking the lock before barging right in.

All three are against the law if the room inside is private. This crime is called 'breaking and entering', even if nothing is stolen.

It is just the same with computers. 'Getting **access**' to someone's computer is a crime. Cyber crime is anything **illegal** to do with computers. Causing harm or stealing through computers is serious cyber crime that now carries a heavy **penalty**. It is also big business.

What is a cyber crime?

- Accessing a computer without permission.
- Stealing information from a computer.
- Sending data that damages a computer system.
- Accessing or sending secret or illegal information.

Word Bank

accessing   getting inside
data   information stored on computers

Cyber criminal

What does a cyber criminal look like? Someone in a mask with a gun? A figure creeping about at night? A teenager sitting at a computer with a cup of coffee in a cosy bedroom?

Believe it or not, they could all be bank robbers. But the last one does not need to leave home. All a cyber criminal needs is a computer. There are no alarms and no car chases. It is all done with a click of the mouse and a few taps on a keyboard. The wires that link up the **World Wide Web** carry billions of bits of **data** around the globe each second. All ready for attack.

Find out later...

What harm can cyber **vandals** do?

What do cyber thieves steal?

What are cyber terrorists?

penalty   punishment for breaking the law
vandal   person who sets out to destroy or damage someone else's property

Very few people owned computers 25 years ago. More people began using them in the 1980s. A few years later, the world entered the **Internet Age**. But cyber crime was already under way.

Even in the 1970s, thieves known as 'phone phreakers' in the USA worked out how to tap into the telephone network. They could make free calls all around the world. This was the beginning of electronic crime. In 1972, a man known as Captain Crunch was caught making free long distance calls. He was sent to prison for **fraud**. Now he runs a computer security company to help protect people from cyber crime.

Sneakers

In 1981, 'Captain Zap' was the first person to be **convicted** of a computer crime. He broke into a US telephone company's computers and changed the timing system. This let him make cheap phone calls during peak hours. He later hacked into military computers and was sent to prison. The 1992 movie *Sneakers*, below, was based on some of his crimes.

Word Bank

fraud   false or dishonest trick to get money
military   the armed forces of a country

The new world

In 1981, the computer company IBM came up with a new type of machine. It was a **stand-alone** machine called a 'personal computer'. PCs were soon used in many work places for storing **data**. Then something big happened. Computers were linked up to 'talk' to other computers across ordinary phone lines.

In 1983 the Internet was first started for universities and the **military**. In the same year, a film came out that gave a grim warning about this new computer world. *Wargames* was about a teenager who broke into a military computer system. He almost caused a world war by mistake. The film showed a scary new world.

Code names

Hacker: someone who uses his or her computer skills to break security for a challenge.

Cracker: someone who often gains access to computer systems to steal.

Sneaker: a person hired to break into computers to test their security.

In the film *Wargames*, Matthew Broderick stars as a teenager who hacks into the US defence system.

Cyber cheating

In 1990, Kevin Poulsen was arrested after hacking into all the phone lines going into a Los Angeles radio station.

The station was giving prizes to the 102nd caller that day. Poulsen made sure it was him. He won a Porsche like the one above. But his luck ran out. The **FBI** caught up with him and he went to prison for **fraud**.

Growing fast

By the mid 1990s, the **Internet** had over 16 million **websites** and was growing fast. This world-wide computer network linked up many smaller networks to make a huge web of links. This became known as the **World Wide Web** (WWW). Information was now speeding around the world like never before. Banks began to deal with huge amounts of money through the Internet.

In 1994, Russian hackers broke into the computers of Citibank. They took more than US $10 million. The ringleader, Vladimir Levin, was arrested in London a year later. Citibank got most of the stolen money back.

Crime wave

Kevin Mitnick of the USA was 17 when he first began hacking. In 1989 he went to prison for stealing **software**. When he was released, he started hacking into computers of **credit card** companies. He stole 20,000 credit card numbers. Once more he was sent to prison for five years. In 2000 he was released from prison. Even though he had caused millions of dollars of damage, he said he had not set out to cause harm.

FBI   Federal Bureau of Investigation, which deals with serious crime in the USA

Kevin Mitnick was arrested in North Carolina, in the USA, in 1999.

Behind bars

In 1994, Kevin Poulsen (below) was sentenced to four years in prison for cyber crimes. He also had to pay US $56,000. It was the longest sentence ever given for hacking. Kevin later pleaded guilty to breaking into FBI computers. He now writes about computer security.

BK

℮ 29384   09·08·90
LOS ANGELES POLICE= JAIL-1

" I am not innocent but I didn't do most of what I was accused of. I never made any money directly from hacking. "

Kevin Mitnick, 2001

software   systems that run computers and allow them to do different tasks

Millennium bug

At midnight on
31 December 1999,
the world held its
breath. Many
people feared all
computers would
crash at the start of
the year 2000 – the
new **millennium**.
They thought the
date change would
close down
networks. Hackers
could then do great
damage. Would the
Internet be lost
forever? Would
banks lose a
fortune? It was
a tense time. But
nothing happened!

Like any house, a computer can be made fairly
secure. But if thieves are determined to get inside,
they will find a way to break in. And once they
are inside, they may:

- steal money to keep for themselves
- steal goods to sell to others
- go round and wreck every room.

Some cyber criminals do just that. They enjoy
wrecking someone else's computer system. Often
they simply want to show off by saying, 'I know
how to cause damage. I've got power. Think
about what I could have done'. Cyber **vandals**
get a buzz from harming the work of others.
They can also do much worse.

Graffiti is a form of
vandalism. It is
spoiling someone
else's property just
like cyber vandals do.

boot sector   program that loads a computer's
operating system

Harmless fun?

Is there any harm in hacking into a **website** to change it slightly? Some cyber criminals think this is just a bit of fun. But what if important information is changed to mislead or upset people?

Some vandals write **software** programs that spread and damage computer systems. These programs are called **viruses**. The results are far from fun. Health and emergency services depend on computers. Cyber vandals could harm lives if they disrupt these services.

Some people think cyber criminals are heroes who 'beat the system'. They think it is clever to bring rich and powerful organizations to a halt. But innocent people often become the victims.

Tricks

Virus writers have learned new tricks. One is to load viruses into a computer's memory so that it keeps running while the computer stays switched on. Another trick is to infect the **boot sector** on floppy disks and **hard disks**. This makes sure the virus gets into the computer's memory straight away.

Cyber vandals put people's lives at risk.

---

hard disk   main storage space and memory on a computer
secure   safe against attack

The worm

Some cyber **vandals** try to **infect** the **software** that computers use. They have developed a special kind of **virus** called a **worm** to do this. When it gets inside a new machine it starts to make lots of copies of itself. The worms keep multiplying as they get sent over the network.

Some worms go into a computer's address book. They get sent as emails to all the stored addresses – without the user's permission. If many computers do this at the same time, the **Internet** becomes overloaded and will crash.

Worms are viruses that spread quickly. They are designed to keep making new copies of themselves. A worm might just get into a computer and leave a silly message or it might destroy the **hard disk**.

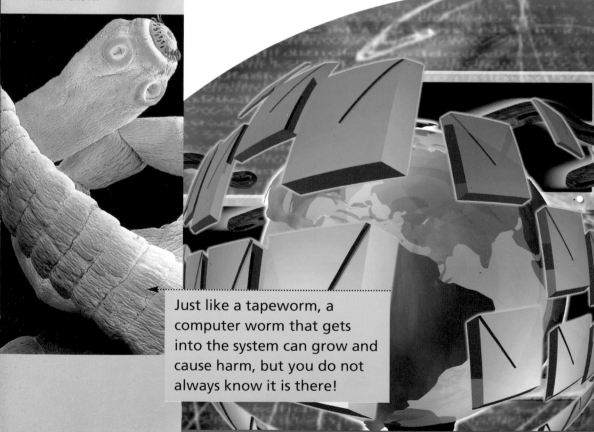

Just like a tapeworm, a computer worm that gets into the system can grow and cause harm, but you do not always know it is there!

infect   pass on something harmful to someone else

An expensive mistake

One of the first worms to hit the Internet began as a program that went wrong. Robert Morris was a university student who was learning about computer science. He created a program that got into the Internet in 1988. 'The Internet Worm' crashed 6000 computers, including a **NASA** network. In 1990, Morris was sentenced to 3 years **probation**. He had to pay a fine of US $10,000.

Morris was one of the first people to be **convicted** under the US Computer **Fraud** and **Abuse** Act. He must have learned a lot from his mistake because today Morris is a computer professor.

Unlike real worms, computer worms travel far and fast.

Did you know?

Another type of cyber vandalism uses a Trojan horse. This is a program that looks like a game or a good piece of software. When you **download** it and run it, it wipes out your hard disk, and your computer becomes useless.

According to **legend**, the Greeks won the Trojan war by hiding in a huge hollow wooden horse. They used this to sneak into the guarded city of Troy and attack.

probation   time of supervision instead of prison, when
behaviour must be good

Just a joke?

Most of us enjoy the odd practical joke. Being teased or fooled for a while can be fun if it is harmless. A hoax can sometimes make us laugh. But sometimes it can go wrong or is cruel. Some computer hoaxes are like this. They set out to cause trouble and panic. Some are against the law.

The hoax

Most computer **hoaxes** turn out to be harmless. But some cost a huge amount of money and cause a lot of stress.

One of the most famous hoaxes to hit computers in 1994 was called Good Times. An email warned people not to open messages with 'Good Times' as the subject. It said that a virus would wipe their computer's entire memory and that they should warn others. Frightened users sent warnings to everyone in their address book. Many **servers** crashed under the strain, which stopped them working.

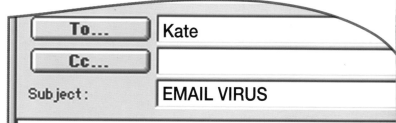

To...	Kate
Cc...	
Subject:	EMAIL VIRUS

Do NOT open emails with 'Good Times' in the subject header

Hi,

Please make sure you do not open emails with 'Good Times' in the subject line as these contain a virus.

This virus will wipe your computer's memory. Please forward this warning to everyone you know.

Thankyou

hoax   practical joke
icon   image or sign on a computer screen

Red Alert

In 1996, computer users began to panic when they got an email alert that warned them not to visit the **Microsoft website**. If they did, their computer would catch a **virus** that would wipe it clean and make it useless. It was called the Red Alert Virus. But the whole thing turned out to be a hoax.

Like a lot of computer hoaxes, it ended with: 'Please pass this message on to as many people as you can'. This is how a lot of hoaxes keep going. Another twist of this hoax came in November 1999. It just said:

DO NOT DOWNLOAD ANYTHING FROM MICROSOFT.

Like the other hoax before it, this was just nonsense.

If people fear their computers are 'invaded' by a virus, they can waste a lot of time trying to get rid of it.

Watch the teddy bear

In 2002, many people were fooled by an email. It told users to **delete** the file 'Jdbgmgr.exe', because it was a harmful virus.

This file has a teddy bear **icon** (below). In fact, the file is an important system file for running the Windows **software**. Without it, computers will not work properly.

Cyber vandalism

Big trouble

In 2000, a 17-year-old Canadian boy (code name Mafia Boy) was found guilty of attacking **websites**. He made over fifty computer attacks, including the websites of Amazon, eBay, Yahoo and CNN. He was lucky. He was sentenced to only 8 months in jail and fined US $250. Most computer vandals face much tougher sentences.

Cyber **vandals** get a buzz from seeing things go wrong. But some like to show off about it, and this is how they end up being caught. Their boasting often gives them away.

There are two sorts of cyber vandal:
- **cyber-punks**: these are usually between 12 and 30 years old. They have grown up with computers and learned their skills early. They often brag online about hacking into systems to vandalize them. Often they do not realize what harm they cause.
- **coders and virus writers**: these people have a lot of programming knowledge and can write viruses that quickly spread across the **Internet**. Coders usually know what damage they will cause.

Mafia Boy arrives at court in Montreal, Canada – unable to show his face.

Word Bank   **anti-virus software**   software that tracks down a computer virus and makes it safe

Spreading like fire

Like some human viruses, a computer virus spreads quickly. Viruses attached to emails can pass around the world in minutes.

Sometimes the computer user has no idea a virus has struck. Sometimes a message appears on the screen on a set date. That might be all it does. Others are far more harmful and are designed to wipe files.

Viruses can soon clog parts of the Internet, as millions of messages flood into a **server** at once. **Anti-virus software** is now big business. Internet users can **download** 'patches' or programs to protect their machines. They are trying to keep one step ahead of the vandals.

Real viruses can grow and spread fast.

The Hacked NetDex.Inc

netdex internet inc.

Complete Internet Services

This Page Has Been Hacked By Analyzer
I hacked this page in order to make things right
Makaveli did NOT hacked any of those DOD systems

The **FBI** website has been attacked by hackers.

Would you believe it?

In 1999, a hacker group called 'phreak.nl' damaged US **websites**. The vandals spread the message 'Hack the Planet'. Another message appeared on the **White House** website. It said in large red letters: 'Hacker wuz Here'. Although this was the only damage done, it showed that even the best security systems could be broken.

The work of the cyber vandals

Virus writers have tried hard to cause **chaos** over the last 20 years. In 1989, only about 30 viruses appeared. Two years later, there were more than a thousand going around the **Internet**.

Vandals release new viruses every day. One of the first viruses to **infect** computers struck in 1987. It was called the 'Jerusalem Virus' and it **deleted** files every Friday the 13th. This day is believed to be unlucky in any month – it was for those who lost important files.

In 1991, a virus called 'Michelangelo' hit the network. It ruined many **hard drives** on 6 March, the birthday of the painter Michelangelo.

David Smith being arrested for cyber crime in 1999.

chaos   utter confusion

Famous names

Cyber vandals were very busy through the 1990s. So were the police.

1992	A teenager who wrote the Satan Bug Virus was arrested in Washington DC. He was too young to be named or to be sent to prison.
1994	Christopher Pile was the first person to go to prison in the UK for writing a virus. He was 18 years old.
1996	'Concept' became the most common virus in the world.
1999	'Melissa' became the fastest virus ever. It caused US $80 million in damage. David Smith from New Jersey admitted writing 'Melissa'. He went to prison for five years.

21st century vandals

The new **millennium** brought new cyber **vandals**. The **virus** known as the 'Love Bug' arrived as an email in May 2000. Everyone wanted to open its message, 'I love you'. This was a big mistake. Love Bug spread so widely that it **infected** 1 in 28 of the world's emails!

Virus causes billions in damage

The I LOVE YOU virus often comes from someone known to the user. It spreads automatically from their computer's address book. The virus destroys files and searches for names and passwords. These are sent back to a secret email address. So far no one has been **convicted** for creating and releasing this virus. The total damage has cost almost US $10 billion.

Re:

Email Virus: Do NOT open emails with "i love you" in the s...

unknown

Fwd: Chinese tradition!! (xx)

Re: Labutis

Saff Memo 04/27/00

bandit   robber or outlaw who belongs to a gang

Warning – 2001

A powerful new Windows computer virus is causing chaos with emails across the world. Experts say the 'Goner' virus is spreading fast. They are warning computer users to delete it. It was first detected in the USA, but experts believe it was created in Europe.

The USA, the UK, France and Australia are the worst hit of the seventeen countries affected so far. Goner can even disable **anti-virus software** in a computer. The rogue email is simply named 'hi' and arrives with an attachment.

Size

How are you? When I saw this screensaver I immediately thought of you. I promise you'll love it.

Do not open this attachment!

05/04/00

05/04/00

05/02/00

04/30/00

04/30/00

04/24/00

Despite the warning, thousands of people opened the 'Love Bug'.

Cyber cafés are getting more and more popular.

Who wrote the Goner virus?

Five Israeli teenagers, one still in middle school, were charged at the end of 2001. 'They are not **bandits**, they are regular kids', said the head of the Israeli police computer crimes squad. 'They are not computer experts, although one of them could write a program. I don't think they fully understood what they were doing.'

The year of the worm

2003 was the year of the **worm**. It was also the year of catching the worm makers.

But no one knows who made the Slammer worm. Also known as the Sapphire worm, Slammer hit the **Internet** on 25 January 2003. It was the fastest-moving cyber attack yet. The number of hits doubled every 8.5 seconds. Slammer did 90 per cent of its damage in the first 10 minutes of its release.

The worm crashed parts of the Internet in South Korea and Japan. It disrupted the phone service in Finland and slowed down airline booking systems, **credit card** networks and bank machines in the USA.

Big worms

In 2003, the Sobig worms began to strike. Sobig F was the sixth version of the worm that infected email programs. It flooded servers and used infected computers to spread itself further. The system could not cope with all the email traffic. One anti-virus company said Sobig F was one of the fastest-spreading worms ever.

Names like Slammer or Blaster describe how fast and furious worms spread outwards – 'exploding' across the Internet.

genius someone with extraordinary ability and skills

Blaster

The Blaster worm was also released in 2003. But there was not just one worm and each type was slightly different. The worms **infected** one in five companies around the world. Helplines to computer companies became clogged and many businesses had to close. Blaster stopped personal computers connecting to the Internet.

People were arrested – each worked alone. In Romania a 24-year-old man was charged with sending out Blaster F. He said it was an accident, but such crimes carry a 15-year prison sentence. An American teenager was arrested for creating the Blaster B worm. The **FBI** had been watching him for some time.

29 August 2003

US TEENAGER HELD OVER EMAIL WORM

An 18-year-old high school student from Minnesota has been charged with creating a Blaster worm. He faces up to 10 years in prison and a fine of $250,000. A neighbour said he was 'a computer **genius**' but not a criminal. His version of the worm infected around 7000 computers.

Cyber theft

Hackers – the movie

In this 1995 film (below), the **FBI** arrest a boy for writing a computer **virus**. He is banned from using a computer until his 18th birthday. Years later, he and his friends uncover a plot by a cyber vandal to release a nasty computer virus. They must find evidence to convince the FBI, while keeping ahead of the criminal.

Cyber **vandals** do not get rich. Cyber thieves may – if they hit the right bank. Some thieves simply hack into a bank to transfer money to their account. Then they withdraw the stolen money.

Other cyber thieves hack into a bank's security files and find account numbers, passwords and **PINs**. If they can steal someone's bank card, they can get cash from any bank at any time. But few people get away with such crimes. Banks notice the movement of money and will soon call the police.

In the James Bond film *Golden Eye*, Alan Cumming plays a computer programmer/hacker.

Word Bank

PIN Personal Identification Number, a code used to get into a bank account

Spying

How useful it would be to get access to the secrets of a **rival** company! If you knew all its plans, you could work out how to beat it. If you could break into their computer records to change a few figures, who would know? Hacking into rival computer files has been going on for years. Even 'just looking' is a form of spying. It is called theft of ideas.

Hacking into a country's defence system to find out its **military** secrets is also cyber spying. Changing a few codes to disable an enemy's missiles or to fire them may not happen only in James Bond films! Today, companies' computer systems can soon **detect** hackers at work.

Mission impossible?

The FBI and **CSI** held a survey of US businesses in 2002. Half of the companies said cyber spying by competitors was a big concern. Thirty-six per cent had suffered electronic break-ins during the past year.

> Rival companies are the single greatest threat in computer crime.
>
> Richard Power of the CSI, 2003

Beware, spies are everywhere.

Daylight robbery

Online banking makes life much easier for people and businesses. But it also makes a thief's life easier too. Computers have opened up a world of big-time **fraud**.

Breaking into computer systems to sell information to criminal groups can make large amounts of money. A hacker just needs to get hold of someone's **credit card** details. To do this, some cyber criminals pretend to be the bank and email a message. They ask the victim to log on to a **website** to confirm card numbers and passwords.

Of course, the website is a **fake** but it looks just like the bank's real one. Anyone who is fooled gives away vital details.

Bank robbers can now work from home!

community service   having to do work to help people in the local area, without being paid

Bedroom thief

Even small-time crooks can get into big-time cyber theft. In 2000, a UK teenager used his computer to find the details of 25,000 credit cards. He posted the details to a website for anyone else to use. In the USA, the **FBI** was soon on to him. The UK police then paid him a visit.

> Mr Gray, 18, was arrested in Wales after an FBI investigation into credit card fraud. He now faces ten charges of **downloading illegal information**, under the Computer Misuse Act of 1990.

Gray pleaded guilty to theft and hacking but said he had not made any money from this. He was sentenced to three years of **community service**.

Australian theft

In a 2003 survey, 47 per cent of Australian companies said they had suffered from cyber crime over the last 2 years.

That was more than North America (41 per cent) and Western Europe (34 per cent). Almost half of these Australian companies were never able to get their money back.

The business centre of Sydney, Australia is under attack from cyber crime.

fake   false, not real

More than a game

Computer games are a multi-million dollar business. Fans keenly wait for each new game to come out. Favourite characters and special effects get better all the time. That is unless thieves get there first.

Fans of the game Half-Life waited for the new Half-Life 2 to come out in October 2003. But it all went wrong. A hacker broke into Valve, the company that makes the game. The thief stole Half-Life 2's **source code**. A **pirate copy** of the new game was then released on the **Internet**. Valve had to stop the game being sold, losing huge sums of money. Fans had to wait for the real game to come out in 2004.

Identity theft

When you log on to a **website**, no one knows who you are. But if a criminal knows your address, **credit card** details and passwords, they can pretend to be you. This is called identity theft.

Cyber criminals steal someone else's identity in order to steal their money or buy things with their bank cards.

pirate copy   version of a CD, DVD or game that has been copied illegally

Copyright

If you write a song or a story, you hope no one copies it and says it belongs to them. After all, they might get paid for it. The law of **copyright** is supposed to protect your work from being used without your permission.

But computers have made breaking copyright laws easy. It is simple to copy all kinds of material with a computer. If your best friend wanted to borrow some **software**, would you lend any of yours? They could then copy it and load it on to their computer. But copying programs and games is **illegal**. Would you still do it?

Downloading information is completely legal on Apple's new online music store.

We have all come to depend on computers. They run our banks, workplaces, transport, power grids, defence, health, police and fire services. If all the computer networks failed, civilization would grind to a halt. If all **hard drives** were wiped clean, the world would plunge into **chaos**. Panic would rule. All **data** would be lost.

Such a nightmare may well be the dream of a criminal in a James Bond film. Some of today's terrorists would take great pleasure in closing down the world's computers. Could they ever do it? Perhaps it is just a matter of time.

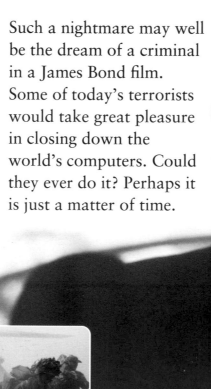

The army respond to cyber attacks as well as **military** crisis on the ground.

Word Bank   al-Qaida   terrorist organization behind attacks in the USA on September 11

Risk of terrorism

Cyber terrorism is the use of computers to scare or harm people. With just a hard drive, **modem** and keyboard, terrorists could control **stock markets**. They could alter government security codes or even take over the world's weapons. Is this just **science fiction**?

Because the **Internet** has no boundaries, an organization such as **al-Qaida** could break into computers from anywhere. It might get hold of top secret information. It could spread messages to scare whoever it wanted. Many governments now take the risk of cyber terrorism very seriously.

In *The Truman Show* a powerful computer network is used to create a fantasy world.

---

modem   electronic device used to connect computers by a telephone line
stock market   buying and selling of stocks and shares

Threats

Threats made to scare people are a form of terrorism. Threats warning a bank that its computer files will be destroyed are a form of cyber terrorism. Terrorists may use **blackmail**: 'If you don't pay up, we will destroy your **data** and tell the world'. Banks might prefer to pay money rather than let people know how **vulnerable** they are. This kind of terrorism has happened, before bank computers had modern security.

From 1993 to 1995, banks in the USA and the UK paid out around £400 million to cyber terrorists. Some only paid after computers were made to crash.

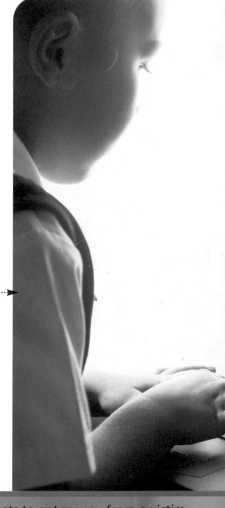

All computers are possible targets of cyber crime.

blackmail   use of threats to get money from a victim

Do not panic

Billions of dollars are being spent on fighting the terror threat. The **FBI** has 1000 'cyber investigators' on the lookout. They have yet to spot a real threat.

Will terrorists swap bombs and bullets for a mouse and **modem**? This is unlikely. Explosions and deaths will always get more attention than cyber attacks. Many security experts think too much fuss is made about cyber threats. What real harm can anyone do? After all, the top-secret **military** computers are not even linked to the **World Wide Web**. No one 'out there' can ever hack into them. Even so, the computer world will always have to stay on its guard.

What if...

Some people fear the worst. What if terrorists break into computers across the world? Could they close down all our power stations? Would the world be left in darkness? What if they break in to hospital records? Could patients be given deadly doses of drugs? This is the stuff of **science fiction**. We hope!

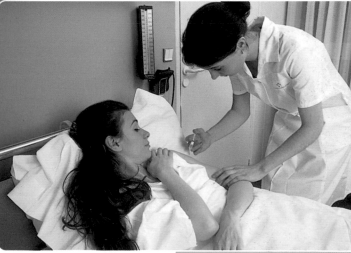

vulnerable   easily harmed or damaged

Big companies and banks were once the main target of cyber crime. Not any more. Anyone with a computer who goes on the **Internet** is at risk. But how can you tell if you are a victim? There may be some tell-tale signs. Has your computer crashed **online**? Has **software** suddenly stopped working properly? Has a file disappeared for no reason? These could be signs that you are under attack.

If you start getting a lot of **spam** emails, you may ask how they all find you. If you find money has disappeared from your bank account, that could be the final proof. It is time to fight back!

Police seize computers of suspected cyber criminals.

Keeping ahead

If your computer slows down on the Internet, keep watch. If you cannot connect to **websites**, hang up and redial. A hacker might be **downloading** files from your computer. Someone out there could be breaking into your system. It may be time to protect your computer with new **software**.

Police are getting better at catching cyber criminals.

deter   put someone off doing a particular thing

The battle

Cyber crime will not go away. It is a growing problem. The challenge is to deal with it and stop it disrupting people's work. It costs countries a fortune and can even be a danger to people's lives. By making cyber crime harder to carry out and easier to **detect**, computer experts hope to make it tougher for criminals. The aim is to prevent crimes happening in the first place.

Punishment

Police across the world are working hard to **deter** cyber criminals. Their message is clear:

- the police are getting better at catching cyber criminals
- the law is getting tougher on those who get caught.

Getting tough

From November 2003, judges in the USA began handing out tougher sentences. Hackers whose crimes result in injury or death now face from 20 years to life in prison. Sentences have now increased by 50 per cent for hackers who share stolen personal **data** with anyone else.

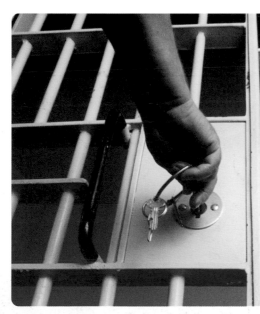

Keeping alert

The great thing about the **Internet** is that it lets people around the world share information and ideas quickly. But such freedom is open to **abuse**. Stricter rules and controls are always being made to keep one step ahead of the criminals.

Fitting better locks and alarms on a house will make it more **secure** against thieves. In the same way, it is wise to fit the latest 'locks' to computers. Updating **anti-virus software** is one way to keep ahead of cyber **vandals**. Another is to fit software called a **firewall**. This is like a guard to keep out emails and **data** that could harm a computer.

Firefighters create firewalls. Like computer firewalls, they aim to keep danger out!

firewall   software to stop certain messages getting into computers from the Internet

One step ahead

Firefighters often burn areas ahead of an advancing fire to stop flames getting through. In the same way, a computer firewall is meant to keep danger out. It should 'burn up' any incoming 'bombs'. If a cyber vandal tries to send you an email bomb, a firewall should keep it from getting into your inbox.

An email bomb is when someone sends you the same email hundreds or thousands of times until your email system crashes.

Even though clever **software** tries to keep out criminals, it might never be 100 per cent crime proof. After all, hackers are always at work, ready to crack their next challenge.

Crime proof?

Security software is like a traffic cop watching cars flow past your gate. It checks each one that slows down or looks like a suspect. But it might not notice the bike squeezing through the hedge round the back!

Keeping to the rules

On a recent poster

Would you go into a store and steal a CD? It's the same thing when people log on to computers and steal our music.

Britney Spears (below)

How easy is it to become a cyber criminal? Many people do not realize they may be doing something **illegal** on their computer. Even trying to guess another person's password is wrong. After all, it is 'entering a computer without permission', which is against the law.

Breaking into someone's email account is also illegal. You need to be careful when using chat rooms and sending emails. Using words or pictures that are racist or **obscene** may be breaking the law. If you **download** or pass on material that others find annoying, untrue or **offensive**, you could also be committing a crime.

Word Bank

culprit   someone guilty of a crime
defence   case to support what you have done

Stealing from artists

Many people download videos or music on the **Internet**. Record companies may let you copy some free samples. Otherwise, it is illegal to copy music. Yet over 2.6 billion music files are downloaded without permission every month.

An MP3 file is a special way of sending music tracks over the Internet. But this has led to 'music piracy' when people swap music instead of buying the CD. It means bands do not sell their music and their work is being stolen. The music industry loses about US $4 billion each year in this way.

If you try to get the latest hits free online, you might be breaking the law.

obscene   indecent material that offends people
offensive   shocking, upsetting or insulting

Keeping safe

So how can ordinary computer users protect themselves from cyber criminals? Although there may only be a few of them out there, it pays to keep on your guard. After all, no one would leave a new car with its doors open and keys in the ignition. Computers, too, need some security and common sense to stop criminals **abusing** them.

Remember:
- Never give people your password and always log off properly after you have finished on a **website**.
- Be careful when using chat rooms. People you chat to are not always who they say they are.
- Never give your address or phone number to anyone you meet on the **Internet**.

Can you believe it?

The **CIA** gave a worrying report. From 1995 to 1998, US government computers were broken in to 250,000 times. These were once prime targets for hackers. Few of the break-ins were **detected** at the time. Security is now much tighter.

It is important to keep your computer secure. You would not leave the doors open on a brand new sports car!

CIA   Central Intelligence Agency of the USA
corporation   large organization or company

More advice

- Never arrange to meet someone you 'chat to' on the Internet.
- If you buy anything **online**, make sure you have full details of the company you are buying from. Keep records of your order and number, in case something goes wrong.
- Never open an email attachment unless you are sure what it is. It is easy to release a **worm** just by opening it. If in doubt, **delete** it straight away.
- If you get an email warning of a **virus,** telling you to send this warning to everyone in your address book – do not! These are usually **hoaxes**. If in doubt, you can check with an Internet security firm.

restriction   rule to stop you doing things

Living proof

Soon you may have to give more than just a password to use a computer. After all, how does the computer know you are not an **impostor**? Before long, machines may need to read your fingerprint (below) before they let you log on. All you will need to do is press your finger against the screen.

What next?

Just 50 years ago, no one could ever have imagined today's cyber world. In another 50 years, who knows how it will have changed? Will cyber crime be a thing of the past? Probably not.

The **Internet** seems to attract people who like to disturb others. From **vandals**, spies or thieves to people who keep sending **nuisance** emails. There are also criminal groups that communicate with others across the world to plot their crimes on the Internet. They include drug dealers, **software** thieves, football hooligans and people with extreme political views who want to **promote** hatred of others. Such crimes are always out there.

Your eye, like your fingerprint, is unique. Reading your eye will tell a computer if it is really you.

impostor   someone who pretends to be someone else
nuisance   causing trouble or annoyance

Future possibilities

Computers may soon **recognize** voices. Or they will study eyes. By reading your **retina** the computer will know if it is really you. Only then will it let you log on.

The Internet continues to be a great learning tool as it opens up new worlds and new ideas. The more people communicate, the more they understand each other. That can only be a good thing. But there is still a tiny fraction of computer users that only see possibilities for greed, mischief or even terror. The cyber world, just like the real world, will sadly never be totally free of crime and the fear it brings.

The last word...

"
The computer industry is working with governments, police and business people to **deter** cyber crime. The challenge is to make sure everyone can use computers safely. This will take a long time, but we must do it.
"

Bill Gates, head of **Microsoft**, 2003

promote   encourage
retina   area at the back of the eyeball

Security

Two-thirds of UK companies have suffered a serious security incident such as hacking, **virus** attacks or **credit card fraud** in the past year.

Hackers are seen as the main threat to cyber security. Former employees and organized crime have also been blamed for some of this crime.

If you want to find out more about the criminal underworld, why not have a look at these books:

Behind the Scenes: Solving a Crime,
    Peter Mellet (Heinemann Library, 1999)
Forensic Files: Investigating Murders,
    Paul Dowswell (Heinemann Library, 2004)
Forensic Files: Investigating Thefts and Heists,
    Alex Woolf (Heinemann Library, 2004)
Just the Facts: Cyber Crime, Neil McIntosh
    (Heinemann Library, 2002)

Did you know?

In Australia it is a crime in some states to:
- own a mattress without a mattress licence
- wear pink hot pants after midday on Sundays
- change a light bulb unless you are an electrician!

Criminal records

- The world's first speeding ticket was issued in the UK in 1896 to a man called Walter Arnold. He was travelling at 8 mph in a 2 mph zone.

- The most successful sniffer dog was a Labrador from the USA called Snag. He found 118 different hoards of hidden drugs worth an amazing £580 million!

- The oldest person to be hanged was 82-year-old Allan Mair in 1843. He was hanged in the UK sitting down because he was unable to stand.

- The world's largest safety-deposit-box robbery took place in 1976. A group of highly-trained criminals stole more than £22 million worth of goods from a bank in the Middle East.

Robbery

Cyber criminals robbed Americans of more than US $437 million in 2003. The most common ways include: using stolen identities, **fake Internet** auctions and dodgy shop-at-home schemes. You have been warned!

Glossary

abuse wrongful use

accessing getting inside

al-Qaida terrorist organization behind attacks in the USA on September 11, 2001

anti-virus software software that tracks down a computer virus and makes it safe

bandit robber or outlaw who belongs to a gang

blackmail use of threats to get money from a victim

boot sector program that loads a computer's operating system

chaos utter confusion

CIA Central Intelligence Agency of the USA

community service having to do work to help people in the local area without being paid

convicted found guilty of committing a crime

copyright law that protects someone's work from being copied by others

corporation large organization or company

credit card plastic card used to buy goods straight away but to pay for them later

CSI Computer Security Institute of the USA

culprit someone guilty of a crime

data information stored on computers

defence case to support what you have done

delete remove or rub out

detect discover a crime

deter put someone off doing a particular thing

download put information from the Internet on to your computer

fake false, not real

FBI Federal Bureau of Investigation, which deals with serious crime in the USA

firewall software to stop certain messages getting into computers from the Internet

fraud false or dishonest trick to get money

genius someone with extraordinary ability and skills

hard disk main storage space and memory on a computer

hard drive computer's main data-storage device that runs the hard disk

hoax practical joke

icon image or sign on a computer screen

illegal against the law

impostor someone who pretends to be someone else

infect pass on something harmful to someone else

Internet worldwide network that links smaller computer networks together

legend story based on possible truth

Microsoft company that made and runs 'Windows' and other major programs

military the armed forces of a country

millennium period of one thousand years

modem electronic device used to connect computers by a telephone line

NASA National Aeronautics and Space Administration (the US space organization)

nuisance causing trouble or annoyance

obscene indecent material that offends people

offensive shocking, upsetting or insulting

online when a computer is linked up 'live' to the Internet

penalty punishment for breaking the law

PIN Personal Identification Number, a code used to get into a bank account

pirate copy version of a CD, DVD or game that has been copied illegally

plagiarism copying someone else's writing or ideas and pretending they are yours

probation time of supervision instead of prison, when behaviour must be good

promote encourage

recognize identify someone

restriction rule to stop you doing things

retina area at the back of the eyeball

rival person or team competing against one another

science fiction made-up stories which may twist the facts of science

secure safe against attack

server central machine that runs a network of computers

software systems that run computers and allow them to do different tasks

source code 'engine' that runs a computer game

spam electronic 'junk mail'

stand-alone computer that is not linked up to any other computer

stock market buying and selling of stocks and shares

vandal person who sets out to destroy or damage someone else's property

virus small piece of software that attaches to a computer program and harms it

vulnerable easily harmed or damaged

website set of pages of information on the Internet about a particular subject

White House government building where the President of the United States of America lives and works

World Wide Web part of the Internet that is easy to search for information

worm small piece of software that enters computers and makes copies of itself

Index